SPORTS ALL-STARS

MICHAEL PHELPS

Jon M. Fishman

Lerner Publications ◆ Minneapolis

Lerner Publications Company
A division of Lerner Publishing Group, Inc.
241 First Avenue North
Minneapolis, MN 55401 USA

For reading levels and more information, look up this title at www.lernerbooks.com.

Main body text set in Albany Std 15/22. Typeface provided by Agfa.

Library of Congress Cataloging-in-Publication Data

The Cataloging-in-Publication Data for *Michael Phelps* is on file at the Library of Congress.
ISBN 978-1-5124-5396-6 (lib. bdg.)
ISBN 978-1-5124-5401-7 (pbk.)
ISBN 978-1-5124-5397-3 (EB pdf)

LC record available at TK

Manufactured in the United States of America
1-42933-26516-9/30/2016

CONTENTS

Rio Gold 4

The Michael Phelps Olympics 9

Eat, Swim, Sleep 16

Star Goals. 20

Swimming Away with History. 24

All-Star Stats 28

Source Notes 29

Glossary 30

Further Information 31

RIO
GOLD

Michael Phelps pushes off the starting block for his first event of the 2016 Olympic Games.

US swimming superstar Michael Phelps was fired up at the 2016 Olympic Games in Rio de Janeiro, Brazil. His toes gripped the **starting block**. Fans cheered and shouted. "When I was on the block, I honestly thought my heart might explode out of my chest," Phelps said. "I was so hyped tonight and so excited."

Phelps and his teammates were swimming in a **relay** race. The 4×100-meter **freestyle** relay was his first event of the Rio Olympics. But Rio wasn't his first Olympic Games. Phelps had already won more Olympic medals than any athlete in history.

Phelps swims his part of the relay and puts his team in the lead.

When teammate Caeleb Dressel finished the first **leg** of the race, Phelps burst into the pool. His long arms pulled him through the water. His legs thrashed behind him. He raced as fast as 6 miles (10 kilometers) per hour. At the end of Phelps's leg, the United States had a big lead.

Phelps after racing his leg of the 4×100-meter freestyle relay at the 2016 Rio Olympics

The United States often wins this Olympic relay. But at the 2012 Olympics in London, England, the French team won the race. They finished less than half a second in front of Phelps and the US team. In Rio, Phelps and his teammates wanted to make up for the loss in London.

Dressel and Phelps had given Team USA a big lead. Ryan Held and Nathan Adrian swam next. Adrian finished the race less than one second before France to win the gold medal. It was the 23rd Olympic medal of Phelps's great career. It was his 19th gold medal, which is an all-time record.

Phelps (*second from right*) and his relay teammates celebrate winning gold medals at the 2016 Rio Olympics.

But Phelps wasn't done yet. He still had five more events to swim at the Rio Olympics. That meant five more chances for gold for the greatest Olympic champion of all time.

Phelps celebrates his eighth gold medal at the Beijing Olympics.

Michael's journey to Olympic glory began in Baltimore, Maryland, where he was born on June 30, 1985. His older sisters swam,

Phelps poses with his sisters, Whitney (*left*) and Hilary (*right*).

so Michael swam too. By the time he was 11 years old, Michael was competing against older kids at the North Baltimore Aquatic Club. Soon he was beating them.

By 2000, 15-year-old Michael was one of the best swimmers in the country. But no one expected a 15-year-old to make the US Olympic team. Then he swam at the **Olympic trials** and shocked everyone. He became the youngest male swimmer to make the US team in 68 years!

Michael swam in just one event at the 2000 Olympics in Sydney, Australia. He finished fifth and didn't earn a medal. While in Sydney, he watched some of the world's best swimmers. Michael wanted to be a superstar just like them.

Michael kept training. He worked harder than ever. In 2001, he swam the 200-meter **butterfly** at an event in Austin, Texas. He won the race in the fastest time

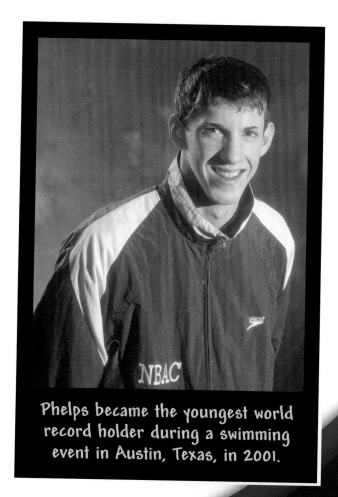

Phelps became the youngest world record holder during a swimming event in Austin, Texas, in 2001.

Phelps claimed a gold medal at the 2004 Olympics in Athens.

Hold your arms out from your sides and have someone measure the distance from fingertip to fingertip. For most people, this distance is the same as their height. But Phelps measures 80 inches (203 centimeters) and he's 76 inches (193 cm) tall. Maybe his extra-long arms help him in the pool!

ever recorded to set a world record. Michael went on a shocking winning streak two years later. He set seven world records in just a few months!

At the 2004 Olympic Games in Athens, Greece, Phelps was big news. He was the most famous US athlete at the Games. He proved that he was also the best swimmer in the world. Phelps earned eight medals—six gold and two bronze. But before the Athens Games had even ended, he was talking about the 2008 Olympic Games in Beijing, China.

People joked that the Beijing Games should have been called the Michael Phelps Olympics. He raced in seven events and won them all. After that, he had just one race left, the 4×100-meter **medley** relay. If he and his team could win it, Phelps would hold the record for most gold medals ever won at an Olympics.

Phelps swam the third part of the relay: the butterfly. When he dove into the water, the US team was in third place. Phelps swam faster than any of the other swimmers. When he finished his leg, the United States had the lead. The fourth swimmer jumped into the pool. He stayed in first place to help his team win the race!

Phelps swims the butterfly in the 4×100-meter medley relay to win his eighth gold medal in Beijing.

With eight gold medals in Beijing, Phelps had become an Olympic legend. Sports fans around the world were amazed by what he had done. "There's so much emotion going through my head and so much excitement," Phelps said. "I kind of just want to see my mom." Phelps found his mom and sisters in the crowd and gave them each a kiss.

Phelps finds his mom in the crowd after a win at the Beijing Olympics.

Phelps prepares for a race at the 2012 Olympics in London.

Olympic swimmers are some of the fittest athletes in the world.

Phelps doesn't want even a tiny bit of body fat to slow him down in the pool. To reach his fitness goals, Phelps works hard—*really* hard.

Phelps swims using paddles during a training session with the US swimming team before the London Olympics.

He says he has time for just three things when training for a **meet**: "Eating, swimming, sleeping, that's pretty much it."

Phelps trains six days a week for five or six hours each day. He may swim as many as 50 miles (80 km) a week. He swims long distances to make his heart and lungs strong. He swims in short bursts to improve his quickness. He practices the strokes he'll use during meets. Phelps also works with gear such as paddles and **buoys**. The gear helps him focus on certain parts of his body to make them stronger.

Swimming 50 miles (80 km) a week takes a long time. Phelps wears waterproof headphones for long swims. He listens to artists such as Lil Wayne, Eminem, and Eric Church.

Phelps pulls weights while training in 2012.

Doctors say most men should eat a little more than 2,000 **calories** a day. Phelps used to eat that much for breakfast. When he trained for the 2004 Olympics, he had as many as *12,000* calories per day. He needed the extra calories to keep his strength up during his long workouts.

Phelps burns a lot of calories while he's training. That's why he eats so much food!

Phelps ate three sandwiches and a five-egg omelet. He downed French toast and coffee. He gobbled pancakes with chocolate chips. All for breakfast! Then he went to the pool and burned the calories. He also burns calories in the weight room. Phelps started strength training after the Athens Olympics. He lifts weights and does push-ups and pull-ups.

He has fewer calories to burn in recent years. Phelps eats less as he grows older. That's because he doesn't spend as much time in the pool as he did when he was younger. He ate fewer than 4,000 calories a day before the 2016 Olympics.

Phelps teaches kids to be safe in the water through the the Michael Phelps Foundation.

In 2008, Michael Phelps had a deal with Speedo. The swimwear company agreed to pay him $1 million if he could tie the all-time record in gold medals. Phelps collected the money after he won

A combination photo shows Phelps with the eight gold medals he won at the Beijing Olympics.

eight gold medals in Beijing to beat the all-time record. Then he gave the money away.

Phelps used the $1 million to start the Michael Phelps Foundation. The group teaches kids about water safety and healthful living. It also asks kids to set goals, which has been a big part of Phelps's success. He also went on a tour to share his message with people across the United States.

Michael Phelps appeared on Saturday Night Live in 2008.

Phelps became one of the world's biggest sports superstars at the Beijing Olympics. Since then, he has appeared on tons of TV shows. He hosted *Saturday Night Live* in 2008. He's been on *Entertainment Tonight*, *Late Night with Jimmy Fallon*, *Good Morning America*, and many other programs. The cover of *Sports Illustrated* magazine has shown Phelps 11 times.

After the 2016 Olympics, Phelps appeared on the TV show *America's Got Talent*. He talked about setting goals and working to reach them. It's what made him an Olympic champion. "I started goal-setting at, like, nine [years old]," he said. "I . . . dreamed for the stars and dreamed for the biggest possible thing I could think of."

Instant Star

Phelps became a father three months before the 2016 Olympic Games. His fiancée, Nicole Johnson, gave birth to a boy named Boomer. Boomer, of course, became an instant star.

Boomer was in the stands for all of his dad's races in Rio. His mom and grandmother, Deborah, cheered for Phelps while Boomer napped or watched. Boomer's red, white, and blue outfits were a hit on the Internet. So were the tiny headphones he wore to protect his ears from the noise of the crowd.

Johnson and Boomer watch Phelps compete.

SWIMMING AWAY
WITH HISTORY

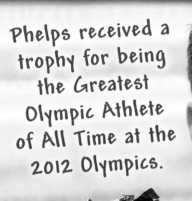

Phelps received a trophy for being the Greatest Olympic Athlete of All Time at the 2012 Olympics.

Phelps won five gold medals at the Rio Olympics. He added a silver medal for an incredible total of 28 career Olympic medals. Many fans believe that number will never be matched. Phelps won't be adding more medals to his collection. He said after Rio that he would retire from swimming.

He has plenty of things to keep him busy on dry land. Bob Bowman coached Phelps for many years. In 2015, Bowman became the coach of the Arizona

Phelps (*left*) and coach Bob Bowman speak at a press conference in Australia in 2014.

Phelps celebrates a win with his fiancée and son at the 2016 Olympics.

State University (ASU) swim team. Phelps plans to help coach the team. He'll live with his family in a home he purchased in Paradise Valley, Arizona. The $2.53 million home has five bedrooms and, of course, a pool.

Phelps and Johnson plan to get married in 2016. They talk about everyday things, such as whether to buy a car or a minivan. They're focused on Boomer. Phelps is excited to spend more time with Boomer and wants to be involved with every part of his life.

Some fans and fellow swimmers don't think Phelps will stay retired. After all, he said he was going to retire in 2012 before getting back in the pool. People often ask him if he's really going to quit this time. "I'm finally ready to retire," Phelps said. "This time, coming back and being able to finish how I did, it was exactly how I wanted to do it."

Most sports fans agree that Michael Phelps is the greatest Olympic champion of all time. Take a look at how he stacks up compared to other great Olympians in total medals won.

Most Individual Medals in Olympic History

Swimming

28 Michael Phelps, United States
12 Jenny Thompson, United States
12 Dana Torres, United States
12 Natalie Coughlin, United States

Gymnastics

18 Larisa Latynina, Soviet Union
15 Nikolay Andrianov, Soviet Untion
13 Boris Shakhlin, Soviet Union
13 Takashi Ono, Japan
12 Sawao Kato, Japan
12 Alexei Nemov, Russia

Biathlon

13 Ole Einar Bjørndalen, Norway

Fencing

13 Edoardo Mangiarotti, Italy

Track and Field

12 Paavo Nurmi, Finland

Cross-Country Skiing

12 Bjørn Dæhlie, Norway

Canoeing

12 Birgit Fischer-Schmidt, East Germany/Germany

Source Notes

5 Childs Walker, "Michael Phelps Wins First Medal of 2016 as U.S. Takes Gold in 4x100 Freestyle Relay," *Baltimore Sun*, August 7, 2016, http://www .baltimoresun.com/sports/olympics/bal-phelps-4x100 -relay-team-wins-medal-20160807-story.html.

15 Associated Press, "Mission Accomplished: Phelps Earns Eighth Gold in Medley Relay," *ESPN*, August 18, 2008, http://www.espn.com/olympics/summer08 /swimming/news/story?id=3538984.

17 Joseph Hooper, "Get into Olympic Shape with Michael Phelps," *Men's Journal*, accessed August 25, 2016, http://www.mensjournal.com/magazine/get -into-olympic-shape-with-michael-phelps-20120803.

23 Erin Jensen, "Michael Phelps on 'America's Got Talent': Boomer Made Olympics 'Different,'" *USA Today*, August 25, 2016, http://www.usatoday.com /story/life/entertainthis/2016/08/25/americas-got -talent-michael-phelps-boomer/89328604/.

27 Steve Helling, "Diaper Bags, Minivans and Marriage: Michael Phelps Tells *People* about His Plans for His Post-Olympic Life," *People*, August 23, 2016, http:// www.people.com/article/olympics-rio-michael-phelps -interview-exclusive-retirement-plans.

buoys: training gear that floats

butterfly: a stroke in which the swimmer swims on his or her chest. The arms move together through the water. The legs kick together in a dolphin kick.

calories: units of energy in food

freestyle: a race in which swimmers can use any swimming stroke they want

leg: one section of a relay race

medley: a race in which swimmers use a variety of strokes—the butterfly, the backstroke, the breaststroke, and the freestyle

meet: a gathering where swimmers race one another

Olympic trials: a competition held a few months before each Olympic Games to determine who will make a country's Olympic team

relay: an event in which teammates take turns swimming, one after the other. For example, in a 4×100-meter relay, each of four team members swims 100 meters.

starting block: a platform at the edge of the pool that a swimmer dives from at the start of a race

Further Information

Fishman, Jon M. *Simone Biles*. Minneapolis: Lerner Publications, 2017.

Herman, Gail. *What Are the Summer Olympics?* New York: Grosset & Dunlap, 2016.

McDowell, Pamela. *Michael Phelps*. New York: AV2, 2014.

Michael Phelps Foundation
http://michaelphelpsfoundation.org

Olympic.org—Michael Phelps
https://www.olympic.org/michael-phelps

SI Kids
http://www.sikids.com

Index

Arizona State University (ASU),
    25–26
Athens, Greece, 13, 19

Baltimore, Maryland, 9
Beijing, China, 13, 15, 21–22
Bowman, Bob, 25
butterfly, 11, 14

freestyle, 5

Johnson, Nicole, 23, 26

London, England, 8

Michael Phelps Foundation, 21

Phelps, Boomer, 23, 26

relay, 5, 8, 14
Rio de Janeiro, Brazil, 5, 8, 23,
    24–25

Sydney, Australia, 11

US Olympic team, 10

Photo Acknowledgments

The images in this book are used with the permission of: © iStockphoto.com/ulimi
(black and white stars); © iStockphoto.com/iconeer (gold and silver stars); DAVID
GRAY/REUTERS/Newscom, p. 2; © epa european pressphoto agency b.v./Alamy,
pp. 4, 7, 25; MICHAEL DALDER/REUTERS/Newscom, p. 6; © Action Plus Sports
Images/Alamy, p. 8; Mark Reis/Colorado Springs Gazette /MCT/Newscom, p. 9;
© Matthew Eisman/WireImage/Getty Images, p. 10; © Donald Miralle/Getty Images
Sport Classic/Getty Images, p. 11; © PCN Photography/Alamy, pp. 12, 16; © ZUMA
Press, Inc./Alamy, pp. 14, 23; 2008 David G. McIntyre/Black Sta/Newscom, p. 15;
© Roger Bacon/REUTERS/Alamy, pp. 17, 21; © dpa picture alliance archive/Alamy,
pp. 18, 19; AP Photo/FEREX, p. 20; © Dana Edelson/2008 NBCUniversal/Getty
Images, p. 22; © Tony Marshall/PA Images/Alamy, p. 24; AP Photo/Matt Slocum, p. 26.

Front cover: DAVID GRAY/REUTERS/Newscom (Michael Phelps); © iStockphoto.
com/neyro2008 (motion lines); © iStockphoto.com/ulimi (black and white stars);
© iStockphoto.com/iconeer (gold and silver stars).